# MARY, QUEEN OF SCOTS

Scotland in 1561 was a wild country. When the young Queen of Scots returned from France, at first her people were pleased to see her. Her husband, the King of France, was dead, and now she wanted a new husband. But Mary, Queen of Scots, was a Catholic Queen, and most of Scotland was now Protestant. There was also a Protestant Queen in England – Elizabeth I. And in those times, men were happy to fight and die for their church.

Who could the young Queen marry? Who were her friends, and who were her enemies? Mary was beautiful and clever. She loved life, she loved adventure, and she loved men. Too many men, perhaps. People said that she was 'mad, bad, and dangerous to know'. But was that really true?

It is 1587, and Mary sits, a tired unhappy woman, in Fotheringhay Castle in England. She is a prisoner of Queen Elizabeth, and soon she will be dead. She takes a pen and begins to write a letter to her son, James, now King of Scotland. It is the story of her life . . .

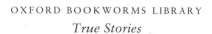

OXFORD BOOKWORMS LIBRARY
*True Stories*

# Mary, Queen of Scots

Stage 1 (400 headwords)

Series Editor: Jennifer Bassett
Founder Editor: Tricia Hedge
Activities Editors: Jennifer Bassett and Alison Baxter

TIM VICARY

# Mary, Queen of Scots

OXFORD UNIVERSITY PRESS

# OXFORD

UNIVERSITY PRESS

Great Clarendon Street, Oxford OX2 6DP

Oxford University Press is a department of the University of Oxford.
It furthers the University's objective of excellence in research, scholarship,
and education by publishing worldwide in

Oxford  New York

Auckland  Cape Town  Dar es Salaam  Hong Kong  Karachi
Kuala Lumpur  Madrid  Melbourne  Mexico City  Nairobi
New Delhi  Shanghai  Taipei  Toronto

With offices in

Argentina  Austria  Brazil  Chile  Czech Republic  France  Greece
Guatemala  Hungary  Italy  Japan  Poland  Portugal  Singapore
South Korea  Switzerland  Thailand  Turkey  Ukraine  Vietnam

OXFORD and OXFORD ENGLISH are registered trade marks of
Oxford University Press in the UK and in certain other countries

ISBN 978 0 19 478909 7

A complete recording of this Bookworms edition of
*Mary, Queen of Scots* is available on audio CD ISBN 978 0 19 478844 1

Printed in Hong Kong

*Illustrated by*: Gay Galsworthy

Word count (main text): 6540 words

For more information on the Oxford Bookworms Library,
visit www.oup.com/elt/bookworms

# CONTENTS

# 1
## Fotheringhay

My name is Bess Curle, but this is not my story. It is the story of my lady Mary, Queen of Scots. She wrote the story, and then she gave it to me. I am going to give it to her son.

She began the story a week ago. It was January 1587, and we sat here in our cold room in Fotheringhay Castle, in the north of England. We couldn't see much from the window. One or two houses, a river, some trees, some horses, and a road. That's all.

The road goes to London, the home of Queen Elizabeth of England. Mary sat with her little dog in her hands and watched it, all day long.

*Mary watched the road, all day long.*

No one came along the road. Nothing happened. I watched Mary, unhappily.

'Please, Your Majesty, come away from that window,' I said. 'It doesn't help. No one is going to come. Queen Elizabeth can't do it – Queens don't kill Queens.'

'Don't they, Bess?' Mary said. 'Then why are we here, in this prison? Why am I not free?'

'Why, Your Majesty? Because Queen Elizabeth is afraid of you.'

'That's right,' Mary said. 'She's afraid of me, and she hates me too. She hates me because I am beautiful, and she is not; because I had three husbands, and she never married. And because many people – good Catholic people in England, France, Scotland, Spain – say that *I*, Mary, am the true Queen of England, not Elizabeth. And Elizabeth has no children, so, when she is dead, my son James . . .'

She came away from the window and stood in front of me. 'James,' she said quietly, 'my son. Does he think about me sometimes? He was only ten months old when I last saw him. It is nearly twenty years . . .'

'Of course he thinks about you, Your Majesty,' I said. 'You write to him often. How can he forget his mother?'

'Then why doesn't he write to me?' Mary asked. 'Does he want me to stay here in an English prison?'

'No, of course not, Your Majesty. But – he has a lot of work, Your Majesty. He is the King of Scotland, and . . .'

'He is *not* the King of Scotland, Bess,' she said. 'Not before I am dead. Remember that.'

'No, Your Majesty, of course not. But perhaps people tell him things that are untrue. You know what people say. Perhaps – perhaps he thinks you killed his father.'

Mary's face went white. She was very angry, and for a minute I was afraid. She said: 'You know that's a lie, Bess. It *is* a lie! I did not kill James's father – I knew nothing about it!'

'*I* know that, Your Majesty. But perhaps James doesn't know it. He hears so many lies, all the time. He needs to know the true story. Why don't you write, and tell him?'

Mary sat down slowly. She looked old and tired. 'All right, Bess,' she said. 'Give me a pen, please. I'm going to write to James, and tell him the true story. You can give it to him when I'm dead.'

'*Dead*, Your Majesty? Don't say that. You aren't going to die.'

Her old, tired eyes looked at me. 'Yes I am, Bess. You know what is going to happen. One day soon, a man is going to bring a letter from Queen Elizabeth. And then her men are going to kill me. But before I die, I would like to write to my son James. I want to tell him the story of my life. So give me a pen, please.'

I gave her a pen. This is what she wrote:

# 2
# France

Dear James. Very soon I am going to die, and meet my God. Before I die, I want to write the true story of my life for you. Everything that I write here is true – I cannot lie to you, or to God. Please believe that, James. It's important to me.

My father died when I was one week old, so I was the Queen of Scots when I was a baby. At first I lived with my mother in Scotland, and then, when I was five, I went to France. My mother was French, but she stayed in Scotland, and died there.

I went to France to marry the King of France's son. His name was Francis, and he was one year younger than me. In 1559, his father died, so Francis was King. Then I was Queen of France, and Queen of Scotland too.

I was very happy in France. Francis, my husband, was like a little brother to me. I think he loved me, but he was very young, and he was often ill. And then, in 1560, he died. He was sixteen years old.

When he died I was very unhappy, and my life was very different. There was a new King and Queen, and I wasn't important in France, any more. But I was still Queen of Scots, so I came back to Scotland. When I arrived in Scotland, I was a young girl of eighteen. My mother was dead, and there was no one there to meet me. I walked off the ship, and I slept in a little house near the sea.

Next day, the Scots lords came from Edinburgh. They were pleased to see me, and for a week everyone was happy. People

*Dear James ...*

smiled at me and sang in the streets. I think everyone liked me. Then, that Sunday, I went to church.

James, my son, you are a Protestant and I am a Catholic. You are a good man, and you love God, but your church and my church are enemies. I was born a Catholic, and I am going to die a Catholic. I love God, too – I hope you understand that. I'm not going to change now.

That Sunday, people shouted angrily in the streets. 'Your Majesty,' said the Scots lords. 'Scotland is a Protestant country. You can't go to a Catholic church here. The Scottish people don't like Catholics.'

'I'm sorry, my lords,' I said. 'But I am your Queen – no one tells me what to do. I don't hate Protestants, and I'm not going to kill them. The people can go to their Protestant churches, and pray to God there. But I'm going to pray with Catholics, in my church.'

People were angry because of that. A man called John Knox came to see me. He was a famous Protestant churchman, but I didn't like him. He was a big, angry man with black clothes. He hated the Catholic church, and wanted all Catholics to leave Scotland. To him, the Protestant church was the only true church of God. He said: 'Your Majesty, you're a young woman, like my daughter. Women can't understand difficult things like God or the church. Find a good Protestant husband, girl. Let him rule this country for you.'

I was very angry with this man Knox. I was a Queen, but I was only eighteen. He didn't talk quietly – he shouted at me. I cried because of his angry words. I could not understand him –

*That Sunday, people shouted angrily in the streets.*

he talked so much, and he knew so many books. But I did not go to his church.

He was right about one thing. Perhaps I could rule Scotland without a man, but I could not have a child without one. And every Queen needs a son or daughter to come after her. So I began to look for a husband.

*He was a big, angry man with black clothes.*

# 3
## Darnley and Riccio

At first I wanted to marry the son of the King of Spain, Don Carlos. But he was a Catholic, of course, and my Scots lords did not like that. It was difficult for me, James. I wanted to please myself. I wanted to please my friends and family in France and to please my people, too. And then there was the Queen of England.

At first I wanted very much to be friends with Elizabeth. We wrote many letters, and talked about a meeting – a meeting between two sister Queens. Elizabeth wrote to me at this time.

*Our two countries need to be friends. You need a husband, I need a friend. Why not marry my friend Robert Dudley, the Earl of Leicester? He is a tall, strong man. I think he could be a good husband for you.*

I was very angry about this letter. There were a lot of stories about Elizabeth and Robert Dudley. They were good friends – he often danced and sang and talked with her. Sometimes, people said, he stayed in her room all night. Dudley had a wife, but one day she died very suddenly. It was an accident – she fell down the stairs, they say. But then, perhaps she was unhappy, because of her husband and Elizabeth.

'And she writes to me about a man like this!' I thought. 'She wants him to marry me, because he is *her* friend – her lover, perhaps! She wants her lover to be King of Scotland!'

I found a better man than Dudley, James. I found Henry Darnley, your father.

He was nineteen years old, and I was twenty-three. He was a tall man, with a beautiful face and big green eyes. He talked and sang well, and I liked dancing with him. He often wore expensive black clothes, and he laughed a lot when he was with me. He was very young and friendly, and I felt happy when I was with him. I liked him very much, and I thought he loved me too.

He was an important man, too. We were cousins – his grandfather was King of Scots, and his great-grandfather was Henry VII of England.

In July 1565, I married him. Elizabeth was very angry, and so were a lot of the Scots lords. My half-brother, the Earl of Moray, tried to stop the marriage. I had to fight him, and he ran south, to England. But I was happy. Your father and I laughed, every day. He was now Henry, King of Scots.

*In July 1565, I married him.*

After one or two weeks, the laughter stopped. A King has a lot of work, James, you know that. He has to read hundreds of letters, talk to people, and think about a lot of important things. I did those things, every day. But now, I thought, I had a man to help me.

'My lord Henry,' I said. 'Would you like to read all the letters with me? You can sit next to me, and you can work with me every day.'

Your father looked unhappy. 'I'm not interested in work like that,' he said. 'I don't understand it.'

'Of course not,' I said. 'You're a young man, my love. But I can teach you.'

For one or two days he sat down with me, and I tried to teach him. But it was true, he was not interested in the work, and he did not try to understand it.

'You do it, Mary,' he said. 'I'm going out with my friends. We're going to ride, and drink, and swim.'

So I did all the work. At night, too, he often went out with his friends in the town. They drank a lot, and laughed and sang, and there were often fights. But no one said anything, because he was the King, my husband. What could people say? They were unhappy, but they were afraid of him. Some of them went to England, to the Earl of Moray.

At this time I was often very tired, because I was pregnant. You, my son James, were alive inside me. But I did all the work of a Queen and I needed friends too. One of these friends was a young Italian, David Riccio.

Riccio was a little man and he was not tall or beautiful or

'You do it, Mary.'

strong. But he was a very clever, interesting man. He wrote many of my letters for me, and helped me. He sang well, too, and I sometimes sang with him in the evenings. I liked him very much, and at first, your father liked him too.

But then, Moray's friends began to talk about me and Riccio. 'David Riccio is in the Queen's rooms every night,' they said to your father. 'She laughs and sings and dances with him, my lord – it is not right! He is not a Scotsman, and he is not her husband. He is always with her.'

Perhaps they said other things, too – I don't know. A lot of Scots lords listened to them. But I tell you, James, before God, I did nothing wrong. David Riccio was a good man. He worked hard, and he helped me – so of course I liked him. Your father did not work – he went out to the town every night with his friends, and drank.

And then one night, your father came home.

*He sang well, too.*

# 4
## The death of David Riccio

It was a Saturday evening in March 1566. I was in Edinburgh with some friends. David Riccio was there, with six or seven other people. We were in a small room, but there was a good dinner on the table, and we were happy. It was dark outside, but inside it was warm and friendly.

Suddenly, a door opened behind me. In the door was Henry Darnley, my husband. I stood up and smiled.

*Suddenly, a door opened behind me.*

'Good evening, my lord,' I said. 'Please come in. Would you like something to eat?'

'No, thank you,' he said. 'I'm not hungry. But I want to sit next to you, wife. Please tell that man to move.'

A man got out of the chair next to me and Darnley sat beside me. Then he put his arms round me. I did not like it. His face was hot, and his eyes looked unhappy. But I smiled and said, 'I'm happy to see you, my lord.'

'Are you, Mary?' He laughed. 'Are you really?'

'Yes, of course, my lord. But —'

Then the second door opened and his friend, Lord Ruthven, stood there. He had a knife in his hand. His face was red, and he looked very angry.

At first no one moved. Then Ruthven said, 'Your Majesty, send David Riccio out of this room, now! I want him!'

I looked at Riccio. He was afraid. 'Why?' I said. 'Why do you want him?'

'He is a bad, wicked man!' Ruthven said. 'Send him *out*!'

'No!' I said. 'You want to kill him. David Riccio is my friend! He stays here, with me!'

'He goes out, woman!' Lord Ruthven said. 'King Henry, hold your wife, please!'

I stood up, but Darnley held my arms and I could not move. David Riccio ran behind me and held my dress. My friends in the room stood up too, and moved towards Ruthven angrily. But he had a knife in his hand.

'Get back!' he said angrily. 'Don't touch me!'

Then five men with knives ran into the little room, and there was a fight. One man held a knife in my face, and another man hit David Riccio, behind me. Then they pulled him out of the room.

'Help me!' he screamed. 'Help me, my Queen – please! They're going to kill me! Don't – aaaaaargh!'

*'Help me!'*

I couldn't help him, because Darnley had me in his arms. But I could hear David Riccio's screams. I think he fell down the stairs, and he screamed for two or three minutes. Then it was quiet.

'What are you doing?' I asked Darnley angrily. 'Riccio is a good man – why are you doing this?'

Darnley laughed. 'You are *my* wife, Mary – not David Riccio's!' he said. 'So why are you with him every evening? You never talk to me!'

'I don't talk to you because you are never here!' I said. 'You are always drinking with your friends! You aren't a king, you're a stupid boy!'

He laughed again. It was not a nice laugh. 'Well,' he said. 'Perhaps I am a boy, but that is better than David Riccio, now. Do you want to go and see him?'

I did see him, five minutes after that. He was very dead, and there was blood all over the floor. Poor David Riccio. He sings to God now, not me.

I looked at Henry Darnley, my husband. He had a stupid smile on his face. But I think he was afraid of me. I looked at him a long time, and the smile went away.

'Remember this night, husband,' I said to him. 'Remember it well. Think about it when you look into my eyes, and before you go to sleep. David Riccio was my friend, and you killed him in front of me. I'm never going to forget that, Henry Darnley. Never!'

*I did see him, five minutes after that.*

# 5
## My son is born

Next morning, Darnley came to see me. He was afraid.

'What's the matter, husband?' I said. 'Why are you crying?'

'Oh Mary, Mary!' he said. 'I'm sorry! I was wrong! I helped those men to kill Riccio, and now the Earl of Moray is back here with them! He hates me! I am afraid they're going to kill me, and you too. Think of our child, Mary, here inside you!'

He took me in his arms again. I was very angry. I am sorry, James, that this man was your father. He was a stupid boy, not a man. He was tall and strong and beautiful but he could never think like a man or a king.

I said, 'You know these men, Henry. What do they want?'

'They – they want our child, Mary. They don't want us. They're going to put you in prison. They don't want you to be Queen – they want your child to be King or Queen. I – I don't know what they want to do with me.'

'Perhaps they want you to be King, too, without me,' I said quietly. 'Then you can do what they say, like a little boy.'

'Perhaps, Mary. They said that, yesterday. But now that Moray's here – I don't know. I'm afraid. Please help me!' He began to cry again. 'What can we do?'

'We can run away,' I said. 'We can leave Edinburgh quickly and quietly, before Ruthven and his men stop us. Be quiet for a minute. I want to think.'

I walked up and down for two or three minutes, then I said: 'Henry, go back to these men. Tell them —'

'No! Mary, please! I can't! I'm afraid of them!'

'Listen to me, Henry! And try to be a man. Go and tell them I'm ill, because of the child. Say I'm not angry with them. Tell them anything – lie to them. Then, tonight, bring some men and horses here, behind the castle . . .'

*'Listen to me, Henry! And try to be a man.'*

He went, and did it. All day I waited in my rooms, and listened. Then, at one o'clock in the morning, Darnley and I went quietly down the stairs behind the castle. Some of my friends were there, with horses for us. Quickly, we rode away into the night.

That was a very bad night. It was dark and cold. I was ill, and Darnley was afraid. 'Come on!' he said. 'Ride faster, woman! You're too slow!'

But I was pregnant, and it was cold and dark. We rode for five hours in the rain. 'I can't, Henry!' I said. 'I'm ill. Think of the baby! I don't want it to die!'

'Why not?' he said. 'We can always make another one!'

I'm sorry, but it is true. Your father said things like that, James. Then he rode away in front of me, into the dark. I rode slowly behind, with my good woman, Bess Curle.

In the morning we arrived at Dunbar Castle. Darnley slept, and I wrote letters to my friends. Next day Lord Bothwell came to help me. I liked him – he was a good, strong man. Soon I had an army of 8,000 men. Bothwell and I rode back to Edinburgh with the army. Lord Ruthven died, and some of his friends ran away. But the Earl of Moray stayed.

All that summer I ruled the country, and waited for the baby. My husband stayed outside my rooms. I did not want to see him. No one did. Perhaps he drank with his friends. I don't know.

And then, on 19th June, in a small room in Edinburgh Castle, my baby was born. It took a long time, but at last you were in my arms, James, my son.

*'Ride faster, woman! You're too slow!'*

I asked your father to come in. 'My Lord Henry,' I said. 'This is our baby! Look at him, my Lord. Take him in your arms. He is your son – isn't he beautiful?'

But your father did not love me, James. Very often, after you were born, he slept with other women. I know that because he talked to everyone about it. I think he wanted people to know. And I am sorry, but I do not think he loved you, James. When I took you to church and gave you your name, he did not come. He wasn't interested.

But because of him, David Riccio was dead. I could never forget that. Never.

# 6
## Kirk o'Field

I had a new man to help me now. The Earl of Bothwell – a strong, clever man. He was older than me; he was not a boy like Darnley. He worked hard and he could think. He was a good fighter and he was not afraid of other men. Perhaps you are like him, James, my son?

In January your father, Darnley, was ill in Glasgow. I went to see him, and took him back to Edinburgh. He was unhappy, and afraid of people. He saw enemies behind every door. Poor stupid boy! He said he loved me again. I was angry, but I felt sorry for him, too. He was very ill.

'It's not far now, Henry,' I said. 'You can sleep in the castle.'

'No, not there, please, Mary!' he said. 'I don't want to go into the castle. I'm afraid of it!'

'But where *do* you want to go?' I asked.

'Find me a little house outside the town, and stay with me there,' he said. 'We can be happy there.'

So I found him a small house called Kirk o'Field, outside Edinburgh. He stayed there, in a room upstairs, and sometimes I slept in a room downstairs. Darnley was often afraid, and I visited him every day. Slowly, he got better.

On Sunday, 9th February, there was a big wedding in Edinburgh. After the wedding, Bothwell and I walked out to Kirk o'Field to see Darnley and talk to him. Everyone sang, and laughed, and was very happy.

At ten o'clock I was tired. 'Good night, my lords,' I said. 'I'm going downstairs to bed.'

Lord Bothwell put his hand on my arm. 'Your Majesty,' he said. 'You can't sleep here now. Don't you remember? People are dancing and singing in town tonight – everyone wants you to go.'

'Oh, yes. I forgot,' I said. 'Of course, people want to see me there. So, good night, Henry. Sleep well.'

Darnley was very unhappy. 'Please, Mary my love, don't go!' he said. 'Don't leave me here!'

But I did not love him now. I remembered the night when Riccio died. So I smiled and said, 'Good night, Henry. Be a man now. Don't be afraid of the dark.'

Then I went downstairs with Lord Bothwell. Outside the house, we met one of Bothwell's men. He looked afraid, and there was something black on his face and hands.

'Jesus, man, how dirty you are!' I said. 'Don't come near me with those hands.'

'No, my lady, of course not,' he said. He looked at Bothwell for a minute, and then ran away quickly. I laughed, got on my horse, and forgot about it.

*I tell you before God, James, I did not kill your father. It was not me. I knew nothing about it – nothing!*

I sang and danced in town, and then went to bed in Edinburgh Castle. Then, at two o'clock in the morning, there was a sudden noise – a very big *BANG!* Everybody heard it all through the town.

'My God!' I said. 'What's that?'

Everyone ran out of their rooms. Lord Bothwell was

*'Jesus, man, how dirty you are!'*

downstairs. 'Don't be afraid, ladies,' he said. 'My men are outside – they're going to see what it is.'

After an hour he came to see me. 'Please sit down, my lady,' he said. 'I have some unhappy news.'

'Yes, my lord. What is it?'

'It's your husband, Lord Darnley. He is dead.'

'But – how? How did he die? Who killed him?'

'I don't know, my lady. That bang – that was his house, Kirk o'Field. It's not there any more.'

'What? And Darnley was inside?'

'Well, no, my lady,' Bothwell said slowly. 'My men found him in the garden, not in the house. He is wearing only nightclothes, and there is no blood on him. But he is dead. I am sorry.'

'Take me out there! I want to see him – now!'

'Yes, my lady.'

I went out to Kirk o'Field in the early morning. There was no house now – no walls, no doors, no windows – nothing. And there in the garden, a long way from the house, was that poor dead boy, my husband.

I did not love him, but I cried then. He was your father, James, and *I did not kill him*. I don't know who killed him, but he had many enemies in Scotland.

I was very afraid. I, too, had enemies, and I often slept there. Perhaps someone wanted to kill me, too.

*And there in the garden was that poor dead boy, my husband.*

# 7
## Bothwell

Soon everyone in Europe heard the news. The Queen of France and the Queen of England wrote angry letters to me. Who killed the King? they asked. I was very unhappy at this time, James. We looked for the killers, but we could not find them. Please believe me, James. The Scots lords are difficult men. Some were friends, some were enemies, but they changed all the time.

Many people in Scotland said: 'Bothwell killed Lord Darnley.' I heard them, outside the castle, and in the town. But I never believed it. People in Edinburgh sold horrible stories and pictures of Bothwell *the same day that Darnley died*. It was too soon. Perhaps Darnley's killers wrote these stories about Bothwell, before they killed Darnley.

I don't think Lord Bothwell killed your father, James. He was a good friend to me in difficult times. He was a good strong, clever man, and he worked hard. I liked that. A lot of women liked him, I think.

Three times that spring, he asked me to marry him. He had a wife, and I could not marry again, so soon. I asked him to wait.

Then, on 24th April, I rode out of Edinburgh to the north. I had five or six friends with me. Six miles outside the town, Lord Bothwell met us, with an army.

'Why are you here, my lord?' I said.

He smiled. 'Because I want to meet you, Mary,' he said. 'I

*'I want you to come with me to my castle.'*

want you to come with me to my castle.' He rode next to me, and his men rode between me and my friends.

I was afraid, and a little excited, too. 'But, my lord, you can't do this!' I said. 'I don't want to come with you now.'

'But I want you, Mary,' he said. 'Your friends can't stop me. I love you, and I want to marry you. What's wrong with that?'

I said nothing. What could I say? I liked him, and he had an army. I had only six friends. So I rode with him to his castle in Dunbar, and stayed there two weeks. And then . . . He was a strong man, and I was only a woman. And I did like him, James. I liked him very much.

*We met them at Carberry Hill.*

After two weeks in Dunbar, Bothwell and I rode back to Edinburgh. His wife did not want him, and was happy to divorce him. So, on 15th May 1567, I married him.

He was a good man, James. A much better man than your father. I needed a strong man to help me rule the country.

But I was wrong. I understand that now. All the Scots lords were afraid of Bothwell, and many of them were his enemies. They had an army, and on 15th June, Bothwell and I rode out to fight them.

We met them at Carberry Hill. It was a hot day, and the two big armies stood, and looked, and waited. Their army had a big flag with a picture of your poor dead father, Darnley, on it. Under the picture, there were the words 'Find my killers, oh God.'

'Come on, my lord,' I said to Bothwell. 'Our army is better than theirs – let's fight them!'

Bothwell rode up and down, and talked to his men. But they didn't want to fight. They talked, and looked at the flag, and waited. Then some of them walked home.

At five o'clock that evening Lord Kirkcaldy rode from his army to talk to us. He said to me, 'My lady, leave your husband, and come with us. We don't want men to die.'

And so, because our men didn't want to fight, I went with him. It was a very bad day for me. They took me back to Edinburgh, and people in the streets screamed at me: 'Kill the woman! She sleeps with her husband's killer! We want James to be King! Kill her now!'

I was unhappy, and afraid, and I was pregnant again. They took me to Lochleven Castle, and put me in a room like a prison. There, I did not eat for two weeks, and Bothwell's children – there were two babies – were born dead. I nearly died too – I was so angry and tired and ill. Then, one day after the babies died, Lord Lindsay gave me a letter. It said:

*I, Mary, Queen of Scots, give the Kingdom of Scotland to my*
*son, James. From today, James is the new King of Scots. But*
*because he is a child, the Earl of Moray, my half-brother, can*
*rule the country for him.*

Because I was afraid, and tired, and ill, I wrote my name on
the letter: *Mary*. But it is not important, James, it doesn't
change anything. *I* am Queen of Scots, not you. That letter
changes nothing.

Bothwell went over the sea, and died in a prison in Denmark.
I was a prisoner in Lochleven for a year. A lot of people in
Europe were angry about that. Queen Elizabeth wrote to the
Earl of Moray. 'You cannot keep a Queen in prison,' she said.
'It is very wrong!' I was pleased about that. But Moray didn't
listen.

Lord Douglas lived in the castle, and his young son, William,
liked me. One day, there was a wedding in the castle. People
sang and danced and drank. William Douglas gave me some
old women's clothes. I put the clothes on, and walked quietly
out of the castle with him. He shut the castle door behind us, to
keep his father's friends in. Then we got on some horses, and
rode away through the night.

All my friends came back to me. Soon I had a big army.
'Mary is our Queen again!' people said. 'Give her back her son!'
You were in Earl Moray's castle, James, so I came to fight him.
I rode with my army to Langside, near Glasgow. And there. . .

There, James . . .

There, my son, I lost the fight. I am so sorry. I had many

good, strong men in my army, but Earl Moray's men were stronger. Many of my men died, and some ran away. After the fight, I ran away too.

I did not want to go to prison again. So I rode south, to England. 'Queen Elizabeth wants to help me,' I thought. 'She understands. She wrote to Moray and she is a Queen, like me. I can come back to Scotland with her army, kill Moray, and find my baby son James. I am in England but I am free. I can try again.'

I was wrong about that, too. Very wrong.

*I walked quietly out of the castle with him.*

## 8
## *England*

Elizabeth didn't give me her army. She put me in prison. You
know this, James – it is the story of your life, not mine. I was
twenty-five years old when I came to England, and I am forty-
five now. Twenty years in English prisons.

Moray told lies about me. *Mary and Bothwell killed Darnley*,
he said. *Mary slept with Riccio and Bothwell and killed her
husband.* But it's not true! They're all lies, James – wicked lies!
They only said these things because I am a woman, and a
Catholic, and they don't want a Catholic queen in Scotland,
they want a Protestant king.

A king like you, James. Why, James my son, don't you help
me? Why are you friendly with Elizabeth, my enemy? You don't
want me back in Scotland, do you? You believe these lies, don't
you? You talk to Moray and his friends, every day. But they lied
about me, James. Moray and his friends killed Riccio. They
killed your father, too. They stole my husband Bothwell, stole
my son . . .

Stole my son's love . . .

I am sorry, James. Forgive me. Sometimes I get very angry. It
is difficult not to be angry, when you are in prison for twenty
years.

Elizabeth didn't know what to do. Sometimes she believed
Moray, sometimes she didn't. She was afraid to kill me, because
I was a Queen. She was afraid to let me go free, because I have

friends in England. The English Catholics want *me* to be Queen of England, not her. And she is a woman with no husband and no son, so she hates me, too.

Sometimes the English Catholics write to me and ask me for help, and sometimes I write to them. Sometimes Elizabeth's men find these letters. The English Protestants want to kill me because of these letters. 'You are a wicked woman!' They say: 'You killed your husband, Darnley, and now you want to kill our Queen Elizabeth. You're going to die!'

'I did not kill my husband,' I said. 'And when I came to England, I did not want to kill your Queen. I asked her for help – I wanted to go back to Scotland! But, my lords, she put me in prison for twenty years! Twenty years, my lords! I want to be free – don't you understand that? When men write to me and try to help me, then yes, sometimes I write back! Why not? Is that wicked, do you think?'

They didn't listen. Of course not. They want to kill me. And so they wrote to Queen Elizabeth. And now I sit here, in Fotheringhay Castle, and wait for her to answer. I do not want to die, James my son, but I do not want to live all my life in an English prison. I am old, and tired of life. Think well of me, James, my son, and . . .

## 9
## *A death*

Queen Mary stopped writing then. Yesterday afternoon, 7th February 1587, we heard a horse outside our window. Mary looked out. There was a man there, on the road from London. He had a letter from the Queen of England.

In the evening, an Englishman, Lord Shrewsbury, came to see Mary. 'I am sorry, my lady,' he said. 'But I have a letter from my Queen. You're going to die, tomorrow.'

*We heard a horse outside our window.*

Mary did not move. 'When?' she asked quietly.

'At half past eight in the morning,' he said. 'I am very sorry, my lady.' He went away.

We did not sleep much that night. We talked and prayed to God, and she gave me her letter to her son, James. 'Give it to him, Bess, please,' she said. 'And tell him how I died.'

'Yes, my lady,' I said. And so now I am going to tell you. King James. This is how your mother died.

At six o'clock she got up, prayed, and dressed. She put on a red petticoat first, then a black dress, and a white veil over the dress. The veil came from her head to her feet; she could see out through it, but we could not see her face. She looked like a woman on her wedding day.

When the Englishmen came we went downstairs with her. Her little dog walked beside her, under the veil, but the Englishmen didn't see that. Six of us went into a big room with her. A hundred people stood and watched.

A Protestant churchman came to talk to her. 'My lady,' he said. 'Pray with me—'

'No,' she said. 'Thank you, but no. I was born a Catholic and I'm going to die a Catholic. I think God understands that.' She prayed for five minutes, and then stood up. The executioner came towards her. He was a big, strong man with an axe, and something black over his face.

'I am sorry, my lady,' he said. 'I don't hate you, but this is my work. Please forgive me.'

'Of course I forgive you,' Mary said. 'I am old, and tired, and you're going to open my prison doors for me. I am going to

*'Give it to him, Bess, please.'*

see God. Do your work well.'

Then she looked at me and her friends. 'Don't cry for me, ladies,' she said. 'Please, don't cry now.'

She could not walk to the block, so the executioner helped her. He took off her white veil, and then he took off her black dress, and put it on the floor. She stood there, in her red petticoat, with a smile on her face. Then the executioner put something over her eyes. Very slowly, Mary put her head on the block.

'The Lord my God is my one true friend,' she said. 'I give my life, oh God, into your hands.'

Then the executioner lifted his axe, once . . . twice . . . oh God! *three times* . . . and her head – her poor, poor head, fell on the floor.

It was very quiet in the room after that. It is a little thing, a head – a very little thing. But there was so much blood – blood on her red petticoat, blood on her black dress and her white veil, blood on the executioner's shoes, blood all over the floor. Blood, blood everywhere.

We all looked, and said nothing. The executioner put down his axe and stood quietly. And then Mary's little dog came out from under her bloody dress and veil, and walked slowly, unhappily, through the blood towards her head.

My lord, the story of your poor mother's life finishes here. We, her friends, cry for her, but that is how your mother died. She died like a Queen. A good lady and a famous Queen.

Mary, Queen of Scots.

*The executioner lifted his axe.*

# GLOSSARY

**army**   all the fighting men (soldiers) of a country

**axe**   a tool for cutting trees and wood

**baby**   a very young child

**bang** *(n)*   a very loud, sudden noise

**believe**   to think that something is true

**block** *(n)*   a big piece of wood or stone

**blood**   the red liquid inside your body

**castle**   a big strong house

**Catholic**   a person who believes in the Christian God and who belongs to the Roman Catholic church (the head of this church is the Pope in Rome)

**church**   a building where people pray to God

**clothes**   shirts, coats, skirts, trousers, etc.

**cousin**   the child of your father's (or mother's) sister or brother

**dance** *(v)*   to move your body to music

**divorce** *(v)*   to finish a marriage

**enemy**   a person who hates you; the opposite of 'friend'

**executioner**   a person who kills people for the queen

**fall** (past tense **fell**)   to go down quickly; to suddenly stop standing

**fight**   to hit someone, to try to hurt someone

**forgive**   to stop being angry with somebody when they do something bad

**God**   the 'person' who made the world

**half-brother**   the son of your mother and a different father, or of your father and a different mother

**hate**   the opposite of 'to love'

**hold** (past tense **held**)   to take something in your hands or arms

**inside**   in

**king**  the most important man in a country

**lady**  a woman

**laughter**  the sound of laughing

**lie** *(n)*  something that is not true

**life**  your life stops when you die

**lord**  an important man

**marry**  to take somebody as your husband or wife

**outside**  not in a building

**petticoat**  something to wear under a skirt or a dress

**pray**  to speak to God

**pregnant**  a pregnant woman has a baby inside her

**prison**  a place for bad people; they must stay there and cannot leave

**Protestant**  a person who believes in the Christian God and who is not a Roman Catholic

**queen**  the most important woman in a country

**ride** (past tense **rode**)  to travel on the back of a horse

**rule**  to control a country (e.g. Queen Elizabeth I ruled England for many years)

**scream** *(n)*  a loud high cry

**shout**  to speak very, very loudly

**sell** (past tense **sold**)  to give something to somebody who pays you money for it

**stairs**  steps that go up and down inside a building

**strong**  a strong man can carry heavy things, does not get tired easily, etc.

**stupid**  not clever

**veil**  a piece of thin material over a woman's face

**wedding**  the day when a man and a woman marry

**wicked**  very, very bad

# Mary, Queen of Scots

## ACTIVITIES

ACTIVITIES

## *Before Reading*

1 Read the story introduction on the first page of the book, and the back cover. How much do you know now about the story? Tick one box for each sentence.

|  | YES | NO |
|---|---|---|
| 1 Mary was a queen when she was a baby. | ☐ | ☐ |
| 2 In 1561 England and Scotland were two different countries. | ☐ | ☐ |
| 3 When she was sixteen, Mary's husband was the King of Scotland. | ☐ | ☐ |
| 4 Mary's son, James, was King of France. | ☐ | ☐ |
| 5 Elizabeth the First was Queen of England. | ☐ | ☐ |
| 6 Mary and Elizabeth were friends. | ☐ | ☐ |
| 7 Mary was a Catholic. | ☐ | ☐ |
| 8 Elizabeth was a Catholic. | ☐ | ☐ |

2 What happens in this story? Can you guess the answers to these questions?

1 How many husbands does Mary have?
2 How many children does Mary have?
3 Who dies first? Mary or Elizabeth?
4 Does someone try to kill Mary? Who?
5 Does Mary get out of Fotheringhay Castle? How?

ACTIVITIES

# *While Reading*

**Read Chapter 1, and then answer these questions.**

1 Why was Mary in prison?
2 How old was Mary's son James at that time?
3 How old was James when Mary last saw him?
4 How often did Mary get letters from James?
5 What lie did people perhaps tell James?

**Read Chapters 2 and 3, and complete these sentences with the names of people in the story.**

1 In 1560, when he was sixteen, _____ died, and so his wife went back to Scotland.
2 The Protestant Scots lords were angry when _____ went to a Catholic church.
3 _____ wanted Mary to marry Robert Dudley, the Earl of Leicester.
4 Mary's second husband was _____, the great-grandson of _____ of England.
5 _____ was Mary's half-brother, and he tried to stop Mary's marriage to _____.
6 Mary had a young Italian friend called _____.
7 _____ helped Mary with her work, but _____ went out drinking every night.

**Before you read Chapter 4 (*The death of David Riccio*), can you guess who kills Riccio? Choose one of these names.**

1  Henry Darnley            4  One of Moray's friends
2  The Earl of Moray        5  One of Darnley's friends
3  John Knox                6  One of Queen Elizabeth's men

**Read Chapters 4 to 6. Choose the best question-word for these questions, and then answer them.**

*Where / Who / Why*

1  . . . asked for David Riccio, with a knife in his hand?
2  . . . couldn't Mary help Riccio?
3  . . . rode away from Edinburgh in the night?
4  . . . came to help Mary in Dunbar Castle?
5  . . . did Mary ride with her army of 8,000 men?
6  . . . was born on 19th June in Edinburgh Castle?
7  . . . did Darnley stay in the house called Kirk o'Field?
8  . . . did Mary sleep that night after the wedding party?
9  . . . did Bothwell's men find Darnley's body?

**Before you read Chapter 7, can you guess what happens next? Tick one box for each sentence.**

|  | YES | NO |
|---|---|---|
| 1  People say that Bothwell killed Darnley. | ☐ | ☐ |
| 2  Mary finds Darnley's killer. | ☐ | ☐ |
| 3  Mary marries a third husband. | ☐ | ☐ |
| 4  Mary loses a fight and runs away to France. | ☐ | ☐ |

**Read Chapters 7 and 8, and then match these halves of sentences.**

1 Mary looked for Darnley's killers, . . .
2 The Scots lords did not like Mary's new husband, . . .
3 The two armies met at Carberry Hill, . . .
4 After Carberry Hill, James was the new King, . . .
5 When Mary lost the fight at Langside, near Glasgow, . . .
6 Mary asked Queen Elizabeth for help, . . .
7 The English Protestants wanted to kill Mary . . .

8 but Bothwell's men did not want to fight.
9 she ran away and rode south to England.
10 so they sent their army to fight Mary and Bothwell.
11 but she could not find them.
12 because the English Catholics wrote letters to her and asked her for help.
13 and the Scots lords put Mary in prison for a year.
14 but Elizabeth put Mary in prison for twenty years.

**Read Chapter 9. Are these sentences true (T) or false (F)? Change the false sentences into true ones.**

1 James came to see his mother before she died.
2 Mary died on a February morning in 1587.
3 Mary was born a Catholic, but died a Protestant.
4 Mary's little dog was under her skirt when they cut her head off.

ACTIVITIES

## *After Reading*

1  **Who's who in this story? Match the names to the sentences below. (There are two sentences for some people.)**

*Lord Bothwell / Henry Darnley / Queen Elizabeth / Mary / Bess Curle / The Earl of Moray / James / David Riccio / John Knox / Lord Ruthven*

1  He was nineteen years old, with a beautiful face and green eyes, and he was Mary's second husband.
2  He was ten months old when he last saw his mother.
3  He was a big, angry Protestant churchman.
4  He was a good fighter, not afraid of other men, and he was not a boy like Darnley.
5  He was Mary's half-brother, and her life was very difficult because of him.
6  He wrote letters for Mary, and he sang well, too.
7  She was afraid of Mary, because Mary had many Catholic friends and they wanted her to be queen.
8  He took Mary to a castle, and married her after he divorced his wife.
9  He didn't love Mary or his son James.
10  She was in prison with Mary and helped her.
11  He and his men killed Riccio for Darnley.
12  She was a queen without a country for twenty years.

2 After Darnley's death, Queen Elizabeth wrote an angry letter to Mary (see page 28). Use these words to complete her letter (one word for each gap).

*angry, husband, killed, killers, marry, quickly, true*

People tell me, madam, that your _____ Darnley is dead. They say that you _____ him, and that you are going to _____ a new husband. Darnley's friends in England are very _____ about this story. Please tell me it is not _____. You must find the _____ very _____.

    Elizabeth

3 Everybody talked about Darnley's death. Here, two men in Edinburgh, Jock and Alex, are talking. Complete their conversation (use as many words as you like).

JOCK: Big news, Alex! The King, Darnley, is dead!

ALEX: Really! When _____?

JOCK: Last night. Did you hear that bang at _____?

ALEX: Yes, I did. What _____?

JOCK: That was his house, Kirk o'Field. It isn't _____.

ALEX: Was Darnley in the house, then?

JOCK: No. They found his body _____.

ALEX: Did somebody _____ with a knife?

JOCK: No. There was _____. But he's dead, all right.

ALEX: So who _____? Was it the Queen?

JOCK: Perhaps. Now she can _____!

4 **What did James say when Bess Curle took his mother's letter to him after her death? Put their conversation in the right order, and write in the speakers' names. Bess speaks first (number 6).**

1 _____ 'Thank you. I must read it later. Tell me, Miss Curle, was my mother afraid to die?'

2 _____ 'She was in prison because she was a dangerous woman! She killed my father, you know!'

3 _____ 'She was forty-five. But she was in prison for twenty years, sir. It's a hard life, in prison.'

4 _____ 'Yes, she was a Catholic, sir, but she was your mother, and she loved you. Please, read her letter.'

5 _____ 'The Earl of Moray told me. I'm sure it's true. He's her half-brother.'

6 _____ 'Here is a letter for you, sir, from your mother. She wrote it just before her death.'

7 _____ 'But, sir, Moray always hated Mary. He tells a lot of lies – please don't listen to him, sir!'

8 _____ 'No, sir! That's not true! Who told you that?'

9 _____ 'I always listen to him. He is a Protestant, like me. My mother was a Catholic.'

10 _____ 'But she wasn't very old, was she?'

11 _____ 'I can't read it now. I have a lot of work today, madam. Goodbye.'

12 _____ 'Not afraid, sir, no. She was tired of life.'

5 Here are some new titles for the nine chapters in the story. Put them in the right order for the story.

- Losing the last fight
- Death on the stairs
- Bess finishes the story
- Death in a garden
- Bess begins the story
- Riding through the night
- Marrying and making friends
- Praying in a Catholic church
- Waiting for a Queen's answer

6 When Mary was a prisoner in England, James did not help her. Why not? How many of these answers do *you* think are good ones?

James did not help his mother because . . .
1 she killed his father.
2 she was a bad mother, a bad queen, and a wicked woman.
3 he did not know her.
4 he did not like her.
5 he was a Protestant and she was a Catholic.
6 he believed all the lies about her.
7 he did not want her back in Scotland because he was now the King.
8 he wanted to be friendly with Queen Elizabeth, and to be King of England when she died.

# ABOUT THE AUTHOR

Tim Vicary is an experienced teacher and writer, and has written several stories for the Oxford Bookworms Library. Many of these are in the Thriller & Adventure series, such as *White Death* (at Stage 1), or in the True Stories series, such as *Mutiny on the Bounty* (also at Stage 1), which is about Captain Bligh and his voyage to the south seas.

In his story about Mary, Queen of Scots, all the characters were real people. Perhaps Mary wrote a letter to her son James, with the true story of her life, but we don't really know. And the question still has no answer. Did Mary kill, or help to kill, her husband Darnley? People still argue about this today.

Tim Vicary has two children, and keeps dogs, cats, and horses. He lives and works in York, in the north of England, and has also published two long novels, *The Blood upon the Rose* and *Cat and Mouse*.

# OXFORD BOOKWORMS LIBRARY

*Classics • Crime & Mystery • Factfiles • Fantasy & Horror*
*Human Interest • Playscripts • Thriller & Adventure*
*True Stories • World Stories*

The OXFORD BOOKWORMS LIBRARY provides enjoyable reading in English, with a wide range of classic and modern fiction, non-fiction, and plays. It includes original and adapted texts in seven carefully graded language stages, which take learners from beginner to advanced level. An overview is given on the next pages.

All Stage 1 titles are available as audio recordings, as well as over eighty other titles from Starter to Stage 6. All Starters and many titles at Stages 1 to 4 are specially recommended for younger learners. Every Bookworm is illustrated, and Starters and Factfiles have full-colour illustrations.

The OXFORD BOOKWORMS LIBRARY also offers extensive support. Each book contains an introduction to the story, notes about the author, a glossary, and activities. Additional resources include tests and worksheets, and answers for these and for the activities in the books. There is advice on running a class library, using audio recordings, and the many ways of using Oxford Bookworms in reading programmes. Resource materials are available on the website <www.oup.com/elt/bookworms>.

The *Oxford Bookworms Collection* is a series for advanced learners. It consists of volumes of short stories by well-known authors, both classic and modern. Texts are not abridged or adapted in any way, but carefully selected to be accessible to the advanced student.

---

You can find details and a full list of titles in the *Oxford Bookworms Library Catalogue* and *Oxford English Language Teaching Catalogues*, and on the website <www.oup.com/elt/bookworms>.

## THE OXFORD BOOKWORMS LIBRARY
## GRADING AND SAMPLE EXTRACTS

### STARTER • 250 HEADWORDS
present simple – present continuous – imperative –
*can/cannot, must* – *going to* (future) – simple gerunds …

Her phone is ringing – but where is it?

Sally gets out of bed and looks in her bag. No phone. She looks under the bed. No phone. Then she looks behind the door. There is her phone. Sally picks up her phone and answers it. ***Sally's Phone***

### STAGE 1 • 400 HEADWORDS
… past simple – coordination with *and*, *but*, *or* –
subordination with *before*, *after*, *when*, *because*, *so* …

I knew him in Persia. He was a famous builder and I worked with him there. For a time I was his friend, but not for long. When he came to Paris, I came after him – I wanted to watch him. He was a very clever, very dangerous man. ***The Phantom of the Opera***

### STAGE 2 • 700 HEADWORDS
… present perfect – *will* (future) – *(don't) have to, must not, could* –
comparison of adjectives – simple *if* clauses – past continuous –
tag questions – *ask/tell* + infinitive …

While I was writing these words in my diary, I decided what to do. I must try to escape. I shall try to get down the wall outside. The window is high above the ground, but I have to try. I shall take some of the gold with me – if I escape, perhaps it will be helpful later. ***Dracula***

### STAGE 3 • 1000 HEADWORDS
*... should, may* – present perfect continuous – *used to* – past perfect –
causative – relative clauses – indirect statements ...

Of course, it was most important that no one should see
Colin, Mary, or Dickon entering the secret garden. So Colin
gave orders to the gardeners that they must all keep away
from that part of the garden in future. *The Secret Garden*

### STAGE 4 • 1400 HEADWORDS
... past perfect continuous – passive (simple forms) –
*would* conditional clauses – indirect questions –
relatives with *where/when* – gerunds after prepositions/phrases ...

I was glad. Now Hyde could not show his face to the world
again. If he did, every honest man in London would be proud
to report him to the police. *Dr Jekyll and Mr Hyde*

### STAGE 5 • 1800 HEADWORDS
... future continuous – future perfect –
passive (modals, continuous forms) –
*would have* conditional clauses – modals + perfect infinitive ...

If he had spoken Estella's name, I would have hit him. I was so
angry with him, and so depressed about my future, that I could
not eat the breakfast. Instead I went straight to the old house.
*Great Expectations*

### STAGE 6 • 2500 HEADWORDS
... passive (infinitives, gerunds) – advanced modal meanings –
clauses of concession, condition

When I stepped up to the piano, I was confident. It was as if I
knew that the prodigy side of me really did exist. And when I
started to play, I was so caught up in how lovely I looked that
I didn't worry how I would sound. *The Joy Luck Club*

BOOKWORMS · TRUE STORIES · STAGE 1

# Ned Kelly: A True Story

## CHRISTINE LINDOP

When he was a boy, he was poor and hungry. When he was a young man, he was still poor and still hungry. He learnt how to steal horses, he learnt how to fight, he learnt how to live – outside the law. Australia in the 1870s was a hard, wild place. Rich people had land, poor people didn't. So the rich got richer, and the poor stayed poor.

Some say Ned Kelly was a bad man. Some say he was a good man but the law was bad. This is the true story of Australia's most famous outlaw.

BOOKWORMS · FANTASY & HORROR · STAGE 1

# The Omega Files – Short Stories

## JENNIFER BASSETT

In EDI (the European Department of Intelligence in Brussels) there are some very secret files – the Omega Files. There are strange, surprising, and sometimes horrible stories in these files, but not many people know about them. You never read about them in the newspapers.

Hawker and Jude know all about the Omega Files, because they work for EDI. They think fast, they move fast, and they learn some very strange things. They go all over the world, asking difficult questions in dangerous places, but they don't always find the answers . . .